WITH GENEROUS H·E·A·R·T·S

How to Raise
Capital Funds for Your Church,
Church School, Church Agency,
or Regional Church Body

Glenn N. Holliman & Barbara L. Holliman

MOREHOUSE PUBLISHING

THE FIRST CHURCH CAPITAL CAMPAIGN

"Then Moses said to all the people, 'This is what the Lord has commanded: All of you who wish to, all those with generous hearts, may bring these offerings to Jehovah...'"

Exodus 35:4-5

Morehouse Publishing

Editorial Office
871 Ethan Allen Highway
Ridgefield, CT 06877

Corporate Office
PO Box 1321
Harrisburg, PA 17105

A catalog record of this book is available from the Library of Congress.

ISBN: 0-8192-1722-0

Printed in the United States of America

TABLE OF CONTENTS

INTRODUCTION

SEVERAL DECADES AGO, I WAS THE CLERK OF THE VESTRY OF THE EPISCOPAL church in a small Tennessee town. We faced what now seems like a modest problem of slightly enlarging our parish hall and repairing a roof and a wall; the estimated cost of everything was less than $20,000. Memory suggests that our annual church budget was close to $60,000, certainly not more than that. At the time, this seemed like a tremendous amount of money, as we vestry members sat around the table and discussed whether we could address these needs or not. After much nail-biting, soul-searching and prayer, the group voted to launch a capital drive.

We managed to do almost everything wrong in that campaign.

- A few of us made all the decisions and failed to share information adequately about the program with the rest of the congregation. An announcement or two was placed in the church bulletin, but there was never any formal meeting to call the congregation together to talk about the needed changes.

- There was no feasibility study to make sure people were in favor of the project and willing to give.

- There was no leadership evaluation to make suggestions as to what giving levels people should consider.

- There were no one-on-one calls. When it came time to raise the money, we wrote letters to everybody—almost the worst thing we could have done. My gift of $500 was one of the largest donations given, and I was a preparatory school teacher.

- We failed to set deadlines.

- Of course, we never asked an experienced fund raising firm or development officer for counsel or advice.

We raised about half of what was needed, and the other half the vestry borrowed. Fortunately, the modest debt was quickly retired, but it was a lesson to me in how not-to-raise funds. Later, I left the classroom and became part of the alumni and development program of the school where I was employed. A few years afterwards, Bishop William E. Sanders asked me to become the Planned Giving Officer for the Episcopal Diocese of Tennessee. Along the way, with training, education, and experience, I acquired the skills necessary to raise financial resources in church, charity, and school environments.

In this book, Barbara Holliman and I want to share with you some of these lessons learned so that you will not be in the position our church leadership was, struggling to do the right thing and not quite sure how to do it. Our group was certainly well meaning, but we could have benefited from advice. In the following pages, we hope you will find counsel and encouragement to help ensure that your next capital drive will be more successful than my first one!

— *Glenn N. Holliman*

CHAPTER ONE

Increasing Competition: The Challenge for the Church

WE IN THE UNITED STATES ARE A GENEROUS PEOPLE. IN THE LATTER PART OF the 1990s we citizens are giving away almost $150 billion a year. Approximately half of this bounty goes to church and religious causes.

However, this $150 billion or so represents less than one-tenth of an annual Federal budget. Government funds—local, state and national—for the arts and human services are being reduced. How will this shortfall be made up? As Uncle Sam cuts back on his Federal budget, people sitting in the congregation, your fellow church members, are under increasing pressure to give away their sometimes scarce resources to these and many other worthy causes.

Ever since our ancestors stepped off the boat, Americans have been trying to build that "city on a hill," seeking to create a utopia. Whenever a problem emerges in American society, we seem to organize and form a group to attack that problem, that disease. This is wonderful. It is who we are as a nation, influenced deeply by Judeo-Christian values.

It also helps to create what is called in the fund raising business, "donor fatigue;" too many agencies and good causes chasing the same donors. This is the way we have constructed our society.

In the United States there are almost 700,000 501c3 organizations, the Internal Revenue Service designation for a not-for-profit agency. Almost 40,000 new 501c3s are created in the United States each year. This is an incredible compliment to the generosity of the American people, but it also represents the staggering reality of increased competition occurring among all not-for-profits. Counting all separate churches, independent schools, lobbying groups, and dozens of other different types of agencies, clubs, and charities, it is estimated that there are almost seven million entities searching for funds. An incredible number of organizations are looking for our dollars!

A century ago, the church was almost the only "charity" in town. The Salvation Army was just getting established in the United States. There were relatively few colleges, museums and hospitals in this country. All has changed, and the competition is going to get more and more intense. One cannot assume that good church members will continue to support the church as fully in the future as in the past. Many thoughtful people believe that they are building the realm of God by supporting counseling centers, homeless shelters, and schools.

Understanding the Basics of Fund Raising

To position your church, ministry, church school, or charity in this myriad of competing not-for-profits, it is important to understand certain terms and the basics of financial resource development. Let us begin by defining four types of fund raising activities: Annual Giving, Capital Campaign, Planned Giving, and the Special Event.

Annual Giving. For a church, these are the donations placed in the collection plate on Sunday mornings, 52 times a year. These gifts finance the ministry, the programs, and the services that churches provide.

For independent schools, charities and numerous of other not-for-profits, annual giving is sought, often by mail and telephone, to underwrite an on-going budget. As with churches, most of our not-for-profit agencies could not exist without this committed and continuous giving.

The Capital Campaign. On these occasions, money is raised for brick and mortar purposes, remodeling, restoration, or church expansion. Donors are encouraged to make pledges, usually for three years or more, without reducing their annual giving at the same time.

Planned Giving. This covers a number of ways that supporters make extraordinary gifts; for example:

- bequests in wills

- life income gifts such as a pooled income fund, charitable remainder trust, or a charitable gift annuity

- life insurance

- real estate

- appreciated property

Planned Giving is one of the fastest growing areas of resource development in North America.

Special Event. Many church people put in a lot of time and energy holding auctions, bazaars, bike-a-thons, barbecues, festivals, or what have you. Many charities and political organizations will hold a fund raising dinner. These are very labor-intensive and often are used to supplement the annual budget or to underwrite a capital drive.

Six Fundamental Steps

Now that we have recognized the competition churches face from secular organizations and have defined some common terms in the fund raising business, let us examine six fundamental steps that encourage giving.

Imagine the annual giving program or capital campaign that you are considering as a wheel or a circle. There are going to be six points on this circle. Think of this as the "real" wheel of fortune.

The "Real" Wheel of Fortune

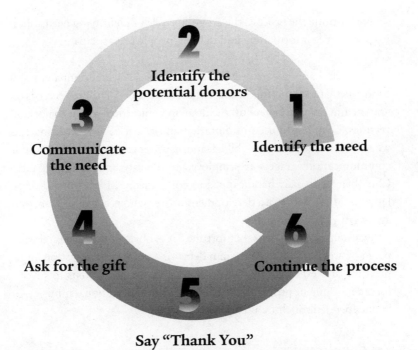

2 Identify the potential donors

3 Communicate the need

1 Identify the need

4 Ask for the gift

6 Continue the process

5 Say "Thank You"

Let us examine these steps one by one:

1. Identify the need, the urgent and compelling cause for which funds are required. What ministries and services are being or would be supported?

2. Identify the potential donors who can financially respond to the need. For a church, this is easy; it is the congregation and possibly those in the community who support outreach services such as soup kitchens or shelters, or historic preservation.

3. Communicate the need to those people who might have an interest in your ministry or program. Do not assume that congregational members fully understand or comprehend the many ministries and programs of the church.

4. Ask for a response, that is a donation to address the urgent and compelling cause.

5. Say "thank you" to those who have made donations.

6. Continue the process, the on-going cycle of identifying needs, sharing basic information, and inviting people to participate.

Successful annual stewardship, annual giving, capital campaigns and fund raising programs follow this "wheel of fortune." The process goes on and on and on and, believe us, the development offices of our major universities, hospitals, museums, libraries, and charities are "revolving this wheel" constantly. Highly skilled and experienced people with sizable communication budgets are employed to identify and encourage gifts. Churches are usually handicapped in comparison. Most churches, even larger ones, do not have a development officer who is engaged in encouraging gift giving to ministry.

By examining the "wheel of fortune," it is obvious that a capital campaign or any fund raising program depends upon communication, organization, and eventually execution. These are necessary steps to success for a development program, be it a church, local or national ministry, or an independent or church school.

Ladder of Fund Raising Effectiveness

At our office, we shudder when the phone rings and someone says, "We are trying to raise several hundred thousand dollars and we wrote everybody a letter, but we only raised a few thousand. What did we do wrong?"

Probably, the first thing this church did wrong was to ignore readiness activities, that is, preparing the congregation for a campaign. One can bet also that leadership failed to do a feasibility study, and most certainly did not follow a standard campaign methodology. But, in addition, the Ladder of Fund Raising Effectiveness was violated. What do we mean by that? At the top rung of the ladder is the most efficient way to raise funds. At the bottom is the most inefficient way.

The Ladder of Fund Raising Effectiveness

1. One-on-one call by a committed person (or persons) on another.

2. Committed person speaks to a committed group.

3. Committed person telephones a committed person.

4. Letter from committed person to a committed person.

5. Committed person speaks to an uncommitted group.

6. Cold telephone call by a committed person to an uncommitted person.

7. Letter and publication by a committed person to an uncommitted person.

8. Print media.

9. Audio and visual media.

To elaborate:

One-on-one. This activity occurs when one or two committed individuals call on another and ask, "Will you join me (or us) in giving?" There's no more effective fund raising event in the world than this simple act of witnessing and asking.

Committed person. Second rung down on the ladder occurs when someone asks a *committed group* to give. Sometimes this happens at church gatherings in which a leader makes an impassioned plea for members to join in giving. It can be very effective and it saves calling on people one-on-one. The downside of this activity is that one is not able to ask people as individuals to consider the appropriate level of giving for their situation.

For example, in the room might be people capable of pledging $1,000 and someone else capable of pledging $25,000. One should call on that $25,000 donor individually and ask him/her to consider one of the leadership gifts. It is very difficult to do this when he or she is sitting with a group. This is fine if you are asking everybody for the same amount of money, but be aware that most groups have individuals who can respond in differing levels of generosity based on where they are in their lives.

Telephone call from the committed to the committed. Third rung down would be a telephone call from one committed person to another committed person. We do not advocate such activity for major gifts, but it often happens as it is convenient. This certainly happens with smaller gifts. Someone might call and say, "Joe, I gave $1,000 last year to your cause. Can you give $1,000 this year to my cause?" It is effective but not nearly as effective as if you call on somebody face to face in their home or office. We repeat, for larger gifts, personal contact must be made!

Letter from committed to committed. Fourth down on the ladder is a letter from a committed individual to another committed individual. It would be similar to a telephone call, and it is best followed up with a telephone call because letters have a way of sitting on a desk and never being answered. Surveys report as much as a five-fold increase in gift support if the telephone call quickly follows the letter. Again, this technique is for smaller gifts.

Committed person to uncommitted group. Next would be an uncommitted group who would be asked by an impassioned person to consider giving. Leaders of charities and political groups often must communicate to "uncommitted" groups the importance of their cause.

Telephone by committed to uncommitted. Following in efficiency, is a telephone call to an uncommitted person by a committed person. These calls usually happen at the dinner hour! Why? Because you are more likely to be home.

Letter by committed to uncommitted. Further along would be a letter from a committed person to an uncommitted person. This is the kind of letter that most of us are used to receiving in our mailbox. Someone has pointed out that, on average, if you are a college graduate in this country, you receive about 300 requests a year to give your money away. Most of these requests come by mail with some form of publication.

Print media. These are ads you see in newspapers and magazines asking you to clip out a coupon or call a toll-free number and give.

Audio and visual media. Finally would be requests through the radio and television in which you are asked to call a toll-free number and to contribute or to mail a donation. Already charities are going on the Internet to encourage gifts from web sites.

In this ladder of fund raising effectiveness, the farther up the ladder you go, the chances of receiving a sizable gift are increased. Spend time in the middle and bottom part of the ladder, and you will raise less money and probably not achieve success in your church capital campaign. To the greatest extent possible, one-on-one calls must be required, and this is one of the major reasons churches employ professional counsel to assist. Volunteers often will not take the time to visit unless prodded and cajoled by management.

With the above basics in mind, let us concentrate now on the capital campaign and learn the methods necessary to achieve the financial goals of your congregation, or other local, regional and national ministries, and church schools.

CHAPTER TWO

The Readiness Phase of Your Church Capital Campaign

A CAPITAL CAMPAIGN CAN BE BROKEN INTO THREE DISTINCTIVE PHASES. THE first phase is *readiness*. The second is the *feasibility study*, and the third is the *campaign* itself.

Let us begin by examining the Readiness Phase. The words mean just what they say, getting ready. The procedure begins when the "vision statement" is created, the reasons that your church or ministry is attempting to do what it is trying to do.

Did you know the Bible records the first church capital campaign? You will find in Exodus, chapters 35 and 36, the first church capital drive. Serving as campaign chairs were Moses and his brother, Aaron. Moses appointed a building committee and a chair, Bezalel, to serve as general superintendent of the project. Bezalel, in turn, appointed a man named Oholiab as his assistant. Together they worked out a plan, giving life to the vision entrusted to Moses and the Hebrew people by God.

Now over 3,000 years have passed since Moses and Aaron labored to prepare their tabernacle in the wilderness, but committees are still struggling to plan, finance, and build churches. If you are a modern-day Bezalel (the supervisor of your building or restoration committee), the following suggestions and shared lessons will help you and your group avoid some of the turmoil experienced by Moses, and by modern-day committees.

Readiness usually begins with informal discussions with leaders of the church recognizing the following sample needs:

- to restore, renew or remodel facilities
- to construct new facilities
- to address programming or outreach concerns
- to build endowment to increase or ensure the continued ministry of the church.

By far, the most common reasons for conducting a capital campaign are to build a new facility and/or to restore or remodel an existing building.

Appoint a Committee

Normally during the Readiness Phase, the leadership of the church authorizes a committee to be formed. This committee is sometimes called an exploratory, building, or a capital needs committee. It is appointed to investigate the problems and opportunities. Usually the first thing this Capital Needs Committee should do is to write a timeline, and outline the tasks necessary in order to deliver a formal report. With this timeline, set deadlines.

Inform the Congregation

Inform the congregation of the creation of the Capital Needs Committee and its purpose through newsletter articles, church bulletins, and announcements from the pulpit. It is never too early to begin a communication plan. You have to tell people what you are going to tell them, then tell them, and then tell them what you told them! You will do this constantly during the life of your program and everyone involved still will not get the message.

Appoint Subcommittees

This Capital Needs Committee then should appoint subcommittees to study the problems and possibilities of construction and/or remodeling. Read the words in Exodus 35:10-12: "Come, all of you who are skilled craftsmen having special talents, and construct what God has commanded us: the Tabernacle tent, and its covering, clasps, frames, bars, pillars and bases..."

As in the Old Testament, your church subcommittees should be composed of skilled crafts people, of individuals who are knowledgeable about construction and/or any of the special purposes of the proposed effort. Opinion makers in the congregation should be asked to serve also.

Involve Others

These subcommittees conduct a preliminary overview of the more obvious needs and opportunities within the church. For example, if the need is restoration, a list should be made of observable structural problems, deferred maintenance, damage, and so forth. Experts should be asked to make preliminary surveys and cost estimates.

Likewise, committees should involve appropriate church members. For example, if a new kitchen is contemplated, those who would use the kitchen should be appointed to the subcommittee. I am reminded of a campaign in a southern state a few years ago, in which a kitchen was designed without input by the men and women who were going to use the facility. There was considerable disappointment about how the kitchen functioned after construction was completed.

Is Christian Education space needed? Then involve the church school superintendent and teachers. In short, those who will work or use anticipated space should have ongoing input along with the building experts in the planning process.

Leadership should bear in mind that major gifts are necessary for the success of any campaign. In many church campaigns, 70–80% or more of the total goal will come from 30% or less of the congregation. In some cases, that ratio increases to as much as 90% of the goal achieved through donations by 10% of the congregation. Therefore, those members of the congregation capable of major gifts should, if possible, be involved in the planning process or, at the very least, be kept informed as the process moves forward.

The key word in any planning process is involvement. Planning, of course, is guided by appropriate committee chairs and the clergy; however, proposed projects must belong to the entire congregation and not just a few. Projects fail if forced from above without "involvement" and eventual "ownership" by those who will be asked to approve and contribute to the forthcoming campaign. This lesson applies to any campaign—church, community, school—any program.

In one church study we know of, there were just a few people who made most of the decisions about the program. When the feasibility study was conducted, it was discovered that the congregation knew almost nothing of what was proposed. Another vestry, we recall, had done all the planning themselves and failed to appoint subcommittees. So when the study was done, it revealed that 50 percent of those who responded had no idea that the church was considering a capital campaign! This is not the way to prepare a congregation for a major effort.

Remember the line from that Paul Newman movie "Cool Hand Luke" of the late 1960s, "What we have here is a failure to communicate." If we fail to communicate, when it comes time to ask people to give, they will fail to make a donation. They will lack information or identity with the program.

Observing deadlines, subcommittees report back to the Capital Needs Committee. The Committee then prepares a preliminary report for the official leadership of the church. The leadership receives the report and may authorize the next steps, one of which may be spending money for architectural plans. Draft architectural plans are then presented to the Committee which pass them along to the official leadership.

Later in this book, we have included a chapter by an architect, Kenneth M. Graves, of San Antonio, Texas, experienced in church and school designs. You should find his advice helpful on what to expect from architects and how best to use their counsel.

Review The Plans

The first estimated costs are projected. After review and revision by the authorized leadership of the church, hold a congregational review of the plans. Some churches will ask the congregation at this time for a vote on whether or not to move ahead in the project; other churches will wait and seek such a vote after a formal Feasibility Study.

Invite, Do Not Command

"Then Moses said to all the people, 'This is what the Lord has commanded: All of you who wish to, all those with generous hearts, may bring these offerings to Jehovah...'" Exodus 35:4-5

We live in a time when there are very few leaders like Moses and it's very difficult in this day and age to "command." In the Readiness Phase, participation, as well as gifts, must be "invited."

Church-wide meetings, forums, cottage meetings, adult Sunday school classes, women's groups, men's groups, by whatever means, use every occasion to inform the congregation of the proposed building plans. Do not neglect to keep informed those who have the capability to make major gifts!

This is a time for prayer. It is a time for meditation. It is a time for quiet reflection and, of course, for continued dialogue.

Some suggested next steps:

■ Publish the projected plans in your newsletter or bulletin.

■ Display the plans (architect's model, drawings, etc.) in the narthex, parish hall, or other appropriate meeting place.

■ Provide detailed explanation about the proposed project by the architect and leadership.

Informal feedback from the congregation should be incorporated into the next revision (which, if many people have been involved to this point, should not be extensive). Major donor prospects must be informed of the plans as the process moves forward.

One can understand from this described readiness process that the use of an architect, the appointment of various committees, and the process of communication may take months, even several years, of preparation and work. Mission statements may have to be fine tuned, space studies have to occur, and many people have to be involved in the process of deciding how to proceed. The readiness phase is critical and cannot be compromised.

Often outside help is needed for the leadership and the congregation to formulate and articulate what they wish to do. This is especially true when the plan incorporates more than the building program. For example, some other considerations:

■ Is outreach to be included?

■ Is money for endowment to be raised?

■ If so, for what categories?

This often involves consultants leading church groups through a facilitation process. Newsprint, a magic marker, and an easel are part of it, as one seeks to put on paper and later into a computer the collective thoughts of the church or other group. Once these thoughts are collected, and these processes have occurred, take it to desktop publishing and lay it out in a format that is easy to read and understand. Now one is ready to engage in the next important step which is called the Feasibility Study.

CHAPTER THREE

The Feasibility Study Phase of Your Church Capital Campaign

OFTEN OUR PHONE RINGS AND SOMEONE ASKS, "OUR CHURCH IS PLANNING A capital campaign; how much money can we expect to raise?" This is often the first question asked by clergy and lay committee chairs.

In the past, a rough rule used to establish the campaign goal was to project an amount that was two to three times the annual pledge and plate offerings to the church. While still useful, beware of such folk wisdom in an age when church members are increasingly under pressure to give to secular capital efforts.

In reality, a church's potential cannot be determined without an accurate feasibility study, a survey of the congregation. If the study does not reveal major gifts, the chance of raising an amount more than one, two, or three times the annual budget is considerably decreased, regardless of the perceived financial wealth of the congregation.

The study is done by a consultant outside the congregation to ascertain the following information:

- Is the congregation supportive of the proposed plans?

- Which components of the proposed plans are considered the highest priority by the congregation?

- Are members willing to support financially the proposed capital campaign?

- What potential leadership gifts are available?

- Is the proposed financial goal attainable?

- When should the campaign be held?

- What additional information should be shared with the congregation?

- Who should be the campaign chair and who should comprise the steering committee?

■ Are Planned Gifts such as bequests in wills, life income gifts, and gifts of real estate, life insurance, and appreciated property possible and appropriate for this campaign?

A Feasibility Study ensures that no one can say in the middle of a campaign, "They did not ask my opinion." It also helps campaign leadership discover if the goals are realistic. Unrealistic financial goals reduce gift support during a campaign as potential donors and leaders discover that there is little chance to fund hoped for plans. Impossible targets make it difficult to recruit workers or for volunteers to make solicitation calls with any enthusiasm. Goals set too high lead to divided leadership and split congregations.

People give to success, not failure. A study is the best way to ensure that plans are acceptable and will be supported by the congregation.

Yet some churches are reluctant to invest in a study. And some capital campaign firms, even to this day, just initiate campaigns and hope the goals can be obtained using standard fund raising methods, along with much prayer and faith. Prayer and faith are important, paramount for a church congregation. However, consider the wisdom found in Luke 14:28-30.

The Carpenter from Nazareth said the following:

"For which of you, intending to build a tower, does not first sit down and estimate the cost, to see whether he has enough to complete it? Otherwise, when he has laid a foundation and is not able to finish, all who see it will begin to ridicule him, saying, 'This fellow began to build and was not able to finish.'"

We do not know any other way to ensure that a modern-day committee can avoid making the mistake of not finishing its "tower" without a thorough Feasibility Study to ascertain financial reality, the readiness of a congregation to give. The lessons in the Bible are there for us to use in this day and age. They speak to us; heed them.

To avoid a debacle as described by Jesus, follow these steps as your church moves toward a capital drive:

1. Pray often, seeking to know and do His will.

2. Plan properly.

3. Employ a good architect.

4. Involve many people.

5. Tell the story over and over and over.

6. Conduct a Feasibility Study.

Some Examples

Let us share with you several stories about studies which we have conducted across the country. We recall one church in the southwestern part of the United States. It was a struggling congregation with a budget of $90,000 a year. A small pre-school was adjacent to the church. The official leadership voted 6 to 5 to authorize a Feasibility Study, testing for $650,000 for capital improvements for both the church and school.

This seemed a large amount of money, given that the church budget was only 1/7th the proposed goal, but we were hoping we would find at least some resources, and plans could be adjusted accordingly.

During the study process, we interviewed one man who said, "I'll give $50,000." Now we thought, maybe $200,000 can be raised.

Then we heard from another individual. She said she, too, would give $50,000. In addition, she wanted to issue a challenge to the church and school. She would give an amount equal to $350,000 if leadership could raise $300,000, more than a one-for-one match!

The church and school rose to the occasion. The total amount was raised, and the plans went forward. Then guess what happened? There were cost overruns. The church went back to the same lady, and she gave another $250,000. This generous woman gave 70 percent of the entire cost of the program!

If there had not been a study, the church and school leadership would not have known that the resources were available to move ahead with an extremely ambitious program.

Another study comes to mind; a strong, middle-class, suburban church in another part of the country. Plans were created totaling $400,000 for remodeling. However, the study revealed that the congregation was ambivalent about the proposed plans and would not give an amount even equal to the annual pledge and plate of the church which, in this case, was approximately $400,000.

We took this information to the official leadership, and they were chagrined that the congregation was unsupportive of what they were trying to do. But at that point in the discussion, several members of the vestry, silent heretofore, expressed their own concerns about the project. The result was that the program did not go forward. Leadership went back to the drawing board and eventually came up with plans that were much more acceptable to the congregation. The moral of the story is plan carefully, communicate, listen to your congregation, accept what they have to say and are willing to give, and adjust accordingly.

Often as a result of a study, plans have to be revised. The financial resources may not be available to support the dreams of the leadership. By all means, have a vision. Just recognize that the vision may have to be divided into phases and done over a longer period of time than initially desired. Certainly it is all right to test for an amount equal to two to six times your annual giving. If you have some potential major gifts, go ahead and share the plans and invite a response. Just be ready to break an ambitious program into parts after the study.

It is important that a congregation feels successful. A study is the only way to ensure that you are dealing with philanthropic reality prior to the beginning of the campaign. God moves in mysterious ways, and often systematically!

What To Do With the Study Results?

Church leadership should receive the study and make a decision on whether to proceed with the campaign or not. Assuming the study is positive, your Capital Needs Committee should recommend the appropriate goal for the project.

If your vision has been too ambitious, it may take time to review what parts of the plan to pursue. Allow time for this process to occur before launching the solicitation of gifts.

For example, we remember several churches where parts of the program depended upon discovering leadership gifts. As these gifts were not discovered in the study, the project had to be altered, parts of it had to be postponed. It took time to go back to the architect and ask for a revision of plans, obtain new cost estimates, and then communicate to the various committees and the church as a whole. In some cases, this process took months, and it was necessary to delay the proposed start of the campaign.

We are good stewards when we listen to the congregation, responding to what they are saying, and, if necessary, altering plans in order to move forward. In some cases, to accomplish the whole program, it may be necessary to borrow money. In the Feasibility Study this should be broached to the congregation, so that members have time to consider the information and to understand what the debt service might do to an annual budget.

Some churches feel very reluctant to borrow, while for others, it is not a problem at all. Do beware of how much you can borrow. Make sure that you are able to repay the debt on a timely schedule, whether it be 5 years or 30 years.

One Midwest church needed a debt reduction campaign, which is generally the most difficult campaign for which to raise funds. This church had overbuilt. Leadership had believed that if they built it, people would come. Well, they did not come and the local economy slipped into a recession. Two-thirds of the annual income of the church had to be used, not for debt retirement, but merely to pay the interest! Programming and ministry were devastated.

So be careful, choose wisely, and do not overcommit yourself in terms of debt retirement. Of course, generally speaking, unless you have cash on hand, you will be borrowing money during the construction phase of your building program.

Once your Readiness Phase and Feasibility Study are complete, you're ready to begin the campaign itself.

CHAPTER FOUR

The Capital Campaign for Your Church

LET US BEGIN BY DIVIDING THE CAMPAIGN INTO FIVE PARTS OR PHASES. THEY are:

- Organization
- Leadership Recruitment
- Advance Gifts
- Congregational Gifts
- Celebration and Acknowledgement

As with any activity, one must assemble people and plans.

PHASE I – ORGANIZATION

A Sample Time Line

Campaigns must begin and end. A thousand separate activities must occur, but here is a "snapshot" of how a typical campaign unfolds.

Month 1

- Establish campaign financial and project goals.
- Set up office.
- Write campaign handbook, including the calendar.
- Recruit leadership.
- Review job descriptions.
- Initiate development of necessary written materials.
- Prepare and begin executing a communications plan.

Month 2

- Complete materials and recruitment of leaders and workers.
- Hold Advance Gift evaluation.
- Train Advance Gift workers.
- Begin solicitation of Advance Gifts and pledges.
- Train Congregational Gift leadership.
- Train Congregational Gift workers.

Month 3

- Hold "Dedication Sunday."
- Hold Kick-Off event.
- Report advance gift pledge total.

Month 4

- Finalize all gift calls.
- Create pledge reminder system.
- Hold "Thanksgiving Sunday" and recognize workers, donors, and leaders.

First, do the mundane thing and set up an office. Install a telephone and a computer with appropriate software for tracking prospects, workers, and solicitation results. Have access to a photocopier and fax machine.

How much secretarial time the campaign will need depends on the size of your church and the size of your financial goals. For some small congregations, only 10–15 hours a week of clerical assistance is required. For larger campaigns and larger congregations, full-time help may be required.

Prepare and publish your campaign plan. Remember, what you are about to do is a communication and management exercise.

Write a Campaign Handbook

The handbook has these key components:

1. An organizational chart.

2. Job descriptions.

3. A time line.

4. A Gifts Essential Chart.

Here is a sample organization chart for a typical church campaign.

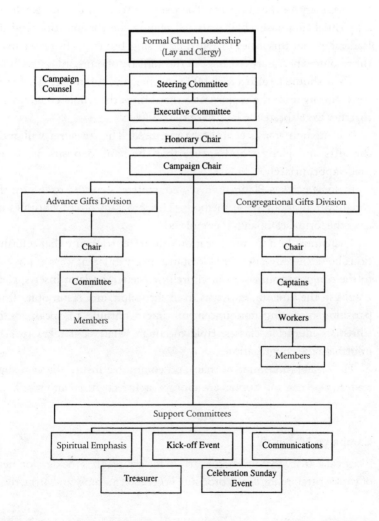

Naturally at the top of your organizational chart, will be clergy leadership, and the campaign chair. Normally, organization will branch off into two sections. One section will be the advance gifts division, including a chair or co-chairs, committee members, and workers to seek the larger gifts. On the other side of the chart will be the congregational gifts division, including a congregational chair or co-chairs, committee members, captains, and the workers who solicit the smaller gifts.

On a few occasions, there should be a community gifts division for those churches, whether through outreach programs or for purposes of historic preservation, that have the ability to reach outside of the congregation for financial support. Also on the chart are the support committees necessary for the campaign. These support committees are as follows: a Spiritual Emphasis chair who will remind the congregation and the leadership that this is not merely fund raising, but is an effort to harvest the resources necessary to carry out the ministry of our Lord Jesus Christ.

There should be also a Kick-off Event chair and committee. These persons will organize the major event that brings the whole congregation together to celebrate the launch of the campaign.

A campaign treasurer must be recruited. The treasurer will audit the gifts and pledges and ensure that the bank deposits are being made appropriately.

In some cases, a Planned Giving committee is created to inform the congregation about these methods. This program often continues on after the formal campaign is completed.

There must be a Communication committee to ensure that information about the program is broadcast in as many different ways as possible to the congregation. Use your church newsletter, bulletin inserts, paragraphs in the bulletin, messages from the pulpit, and testimonies from parishioners during announcement time. Continue to speak to the Christian education classes. Hold meetings; whatever it takes to keep informing the congregation.

The Celebration Sunday chair and committee insure the campaign leaders, workers, and donors are appropriately recognized and thanked.

Campaign Materials

A critical activity that will occur early in the campaign is the development of your written materials. A brochure is needed to simply and attractively describe the campaign goals. Some, especially the inner circle, know what the campaign is about, but the rest of the congregation needs to be informed. In just a few pages, articulate why your church needs to raise money to build or restore. Include photographs and, if appropriate to the size of the project, drawings or architectural renderings. Also, the Gifts Essential Chart, the campaign prayer, and names and roles of leadership are included.

This is the chance to answer some of the hard questions revealed in the feasibility study and to celebrate the good news of the ministry you are trying to advance. Certain important elements need to be included, one of the most significant being a "Gifts Essential Chart." These sample charts suggest the giving levels necessary in order to achieve your campaign goal.

A SAMPLE GIFTS ESSENTIAL CHART

1. For a goal of $500,000 (for a church with 300–400 families)

Size of gift	# Needed	Cumulative Total
$75,000	1	$75,000
50,000	1	125,000
25,000	2	175,000
10,000	3	205,000
5,000	10	255,000
3,000	30	345,000
1,000	100	445,000
Below $1,000	Many	Goal Achieved

2. For a goal of $500,000 (for a church with 100–200 families)

Size of gift	# Needed	Cumulative Total
$100,000	1	$100,000
75,000	1	175,000
50,000	1	225,000
25,000	1	250,000
10,000	5	300,000
5,000	10	350,000
3,000	25	425,000
1,000	50	475,000
Below $1,000	Many	Goal Achieved

If you desire an audiovisual for your campaign, as some of the larger campaigns do, then it is past time to get started on that activity. Do expect Murphy's Law to take over. A good brochure may take you anywhere from three to six weeks to prepare from beginning to end; a video even longer. Both are labor-intensive efforts.

How extensive a brochure should be varies. Some smaller campaigns merely have four pages put together on desktop publishing. More involved, larger campaigns, may require more elaborate brochures to describe what is happening. Of course, there must be a pledge card and other materials such as the worker solicitation training leaflet.

The pledge card is important. Normally the following items are included, often on a four, rather than a two panel, card:

- Space for name, address and telephone number. Newer cards also allow space for fax and e-mail addresses.

- Space for the amount of the pledge, amount paid with this card (if any), and remaining outstanding balance.

- Indication of donation schedule such as weekly, monthly, quarterly, or annually.

- The Gifts Essential Chart (which reminds donors of what gifts are necessary to achieve success).

- The campaign prayer and any accompanying scripture.

- The campaign theme and logo.

The paper stock and colors of the pledge card, in fact all materials, should complement the campaign brochure.

Phase II – Leadership Recruitment

Remember those job descriptions and the organization chart. Recruit these individuals to assume committee chair positions and ask them to begin working and recruiting their own captains and workers. Recruit the Advance Gifts Chair and ask him/her to appoint an Advance Gifts Committee, a committee that will help evaluate each family unit in your congregation to ascertain an estimate of their ability to make major gifts. The Advance Gifts Chair is critical. This person must be able to make a sizeable gift and have the ability to ask others to make large gifts. Remember, financial peers call on financial peers.

This advance gifts evaluation is absolutely critical to the success of the program. Many church committees will not carry out this crucial exercise unless there is outside counsel to insist and ensure that they literally go through the church directory and estimate what people should be asked to consider as a gift. Some people feel uncomfortable doing this exercise, but it is absolutely essential and critical to the success of most programs. This evaluation is based on the giving range estimated during the feasibility study, their annual stewardship gift, or donations made to other organizations.

People are looking for guidance as to the appropriate size of their gift. Often they will ask the caller one or both of these questions: "What did you do?" and/or "What do you want me to do?" This evaluation provides the guidelines needed by volunteers, and is critical in the Advance Gift Phase.

One does not simply go to people and ask, "Would you make a gift?" One asks:

- "Can you consider a leadership gift?" (referring to the Gifts Essential Chart in the brochure), or

- "Can you consider joining me in the range of such and such?" or

- "I am making a gift in the range of such and such. Would you consider the same giving level?"

This is important. Most people welcome the knowledge about what they should consider in order to accomplish the church goal. If you do not suggest a giving level, human nature will take over and people will give less than is going to be necessary to achieve success in your campaign. People want to do what is appropriate, and are looking for guidance from the solicitor!

The second category for which to recruit leadership is the Congregational Gifts Division. This division includes the smaller gifts, and usually many workers must be recruited to ensure that all the cards are worked.

Phase III – Advance Gifts

This phase is called Advance Gifts solicitation. Just as in any community or charity campaign, leaders must go to a certain percentage of the church population early and ask for their consideration of a major gift. Most people know when they are asked early in a campaign, that they are expected to consider the leadership gifts. These gifts are important. They will ensure the success of your campaign and provide the momentum that is so very important to encourage the rest of the congregation.

The reality for most church campaigns is that a handful of donors will give an amount equal to half or more of the financial goal. In almost all cases, 75% to 80% of all giving totals will come from 20% to 25% of the congregation. For campaigns with sizeable goals, as few as 5% to 10% of the donors will give an amount equal to 90% or 95% of the goal!

Time after time someone new to capital campaigning will suggest that if each family unit gave such an amount, we could raise such and such. It never works like that. Some people have been blessed with sizeable worldly assets; others have not. Some are supporting major pledges in other campaigns and cannot give to this one. Others may not be able, for family and economic reasons, to give at all. Still others may not embrace the campaign projects.

How many people fall into the Advance Gifts category? That depends upon your church and on how "advance gift" is defined. Generally speaking, anyone who has the capability of making a minimum gift of $3,000–$5,000 or more over a three-year pledge payment period usually falls into what is called the "advance gift" category. Normally, but not always, about 15–25% of a middle class congregation will fall into this category.

It is necessary to have a separate division. This group sets the momentum for the campaign and raises usually 80% or more of the goal. When you launch the campaign at the Kick-off Event, you will announce the amount raised by the Advance Gifts Division. The goal now appears achievable to the remainder of the congregation that has not yet been approached.

Be aware of the Rule of Five: "One person calls on five others." If, for example, your church has 100 families, 20 to 25 may fall into the "Advance Gifts" category. You will need about five workers to call on the 20–25 individual units. These workers visit early, and take the materials that have been prepared. Stress regular report meetings, weekly if possible, at the same time, same place. Your leadership is present to receive reports from workers on the status of their personal calls to the prospects.

This is critical. Fail to have a weekly meeting and you will soon find the campaign falling behind schedule. Here campaign counsel is instrumental in setting deadlines, ensuring that they are met, and providing discipline. It is important to have regular communications, such as a weekly memo to all workers, with telephone follow-up. Do be aware that approximately one out of every three workers, whether in the Advance Gifts or Congregational Gifts division, will not make their calls. It will be necessary for campaign leadership to reassign these unworked cards as you move through your weekly meetings to ensure that people are called upon.

Deadline setting is important. Do not let the campaign bog down. The longer the card is out, usually it loses gift value.

Worker Orientation and Training

During this phase, conduct the first worker training session for the major gifts. The worker training session is critical.

Basically the agenda for worker orientation and training is as follows:

1. Open with prayer seeking to do God's will.

2. Remind workers what the campaign is about.

3. Describe the organization campaign plan and time line.

4. Inform what is expected of them.

5. Conduct role playing exercises on "How to Ask for a Gift."

6. Ask them to select prospect cards for solicitation.

7. Record the cards that each worker takes.

8. Set dates for worker reporting.

Use your campaign handbook, which you developed in Phase I, to share with people what must happen and when.

Record Gifts

As gifts are received, it is necessary to record these gifts. The campaign assistant records the pledges. The campaign treasurer makes the deposits. Thank you letters should go out as quickly as possible after the pledge or gift is made. Later, reminder notices must be sent. These should be in the form of a letter with an update on the progress of the project.

It is absolutely critical to track every pledge card. Failure to track pledge cards, to keep up with who has what card, is a recipe for disaster. Your church will not be as successful as it could have been.

Phase IV – Congregational Gifts

This is the smaller gift phase. The Advance Gifts workers have been working for several weeks and gifts and pledges are on hand. Your campaign is now ready for the official kick-off weekend and the solicitation of all remaining members of the congregation.

The official kick-off involves a Dedication Sunday in which the congregation, with a special liturgy and prayers, dedicate themselves to the task at hand. During the service, commission all workers with a liturgy where they are recognized as the workers who will be making personal calls on fellow parishioners.

Generally we find about 75% to 85% of a middle class congregation will fall into the Congregational Gifts phase. This means people capable of giving donations anywhere from $25 to as high as $3,000 or even more. There will be more individuals in this category which means that one will need more workers. Again, use the Rule of Five; one worker takes five cards.

For example, your church has 100 potential giving units, 20 of whom have fallen into the Advance Gifts category. Then 80 cards will be available in the next category. Eighty divided by five suggests a need for 16 workers. Always try to recruit a few more than needed because some people (as many as one-third or more) will not work their cards or something will happen and prospects will be out of town and the workers are unable to accomplish their calls in a timely fashion.

Of course, workers attend the Congregational Gifts Worker Orientation and Training Session to select their pledge cards, to learn more about the campaign, to receive their materials, and to be inspired to go forth and visit their fellow individuals. This session occurs either a few days before or after Dedication Sunday and the Kick-off Event.

The Kick-off Event is a critical and festive event. It usually involves some type of meal. It is the "Great Coming Together." If one were a physicist, one would say, "We were entering into critical mass," in which we literally have to "explode" the campaign on the congregation.

What type of event should you have? That depends upon the culture of your church. Some churches go to a big hotel or a country club for a dinner; others have a picnic on the grounds; and still, for others, it is a catered affair in the parish or fellowship hall. Whatever suits your culture, work at it very hard, and make this very special. If appropriate, invite guests or religious leaders to come and help give some added excitement. Have music! Invite former clergy! Try to have there everybody possible who has impacted positively on the life of the church. Run special vans to pick up the elderly and shut-ins, and provide child care service so young parents can attend. The highlight of the program at this event is the announcement of the total Advance Gifts raised to date. Usually, this is about 50% to 60% of the total goal. This exciting announcement raises the sights and enthusiasm of the members.

Do not charge for this event. Some people think if they give $25 for the dinner, they have made their gift to the campaign. Do not fall into this trap. Allocate money in the campaign budget for this activity; you will get your money back many, many times over. If you fail to have a kick-off event, you will find it much more difficult to get people to give to the campaign. They simply will not have focused. The campaign will be just another ordinary fund drive in their busy lives rather than an important, special episode which heightened their awareness and interest in the project and the church.

Phase V – Celebration and Acknowledgment

Depending on the size of your congregation, it will take a number of weeks for workers to make their calls. Again, conduct weekly report meetings, and, as the reports come in, the campaign secretary continues to send out the acknowledgment and letters signed by the appropriate campaign leadership. The gifts are recorded and deposits are made. The campaign, in a short period of time, will come to a formal end in terms of the solicitation.

Consider the appointment of an ongoing Post-Capital Campaign Review Committee as the drive concludes. This committee should meet quarterly to evaluate how the pledge collection is proceeding, discover what the attrition rate is, and do what is necessary to encourage that attrition be held as low as possible.

The campaign comes to a formal conclusion, but there still needs to be regular communication telling people how wisely the church is using their funds over the life of the pledge pay out period. For example, when it is ground-breaking time, make sure that everybody is invited to the event, and ensure you have regular announcements in your bulletins and newsletters about the progress of the projects funded. Make both oral and written communications about how plans are proceeding, and attrition will be kept to a minimum.

You should schedule a concluding event. Plan a Sunday of Thanksgiving in which, through prayer, song, and spoken words, the good news is announced that additional ministry is enabled because of the generosity of the congregation in the effort just concluded. Recognize the volunteer leadership for their participation.

It may take three to four months to conduct your campaign from beginning to end if you are a medium-sized church. It will take perhaps three to five years for all the pledges to be collected.

Generally speaking, within the first year, you will receive about 35% to 40% of all your gifts from the pledges. Year two, expect to receive 25% to 30% of your gift total. Year three, you might receive 20% to 25% percent of your gift total. The remaining amount to be collected will trickle in during years four and five.

Expect some attrition, approximately 5% for a church campaign. People move, pass away, get angry, and change churches–that just happens. The more efficient you can be in sending out reminder notices and celebrating the good works that occur as a result of the generosity from the congregation, the more attrition can be held to a minimum.

CHAPTER FIVE

Common Questions About a Church Capital Campaign

THE QUESTION IS OFTEN ASKED, "CAN WE GO OUTSIDE OF THE CONGREGATION to raise funds?" The short answer is usually "no." The longer answer is "sometimes." Generally speaking, businesses, corporations, and most foundations, cannot or will not give for religious causes.

However, if your church has a significant outreach program that serves the community, has a day school associated with the campaign, or a day-care center that serves the community, you may be able to interpret your church to the public as a community resource. These programs provide the leverage necessary to approach these individuals, corporations, companies, and foundations who would not normally give for a church cause.

We are reminded of a church in New York City that was, in essence, the community center for the neighborhood. Young people in the area utilized the center during the day and the adults at night. It was a wonderful ministry but the church was literally wearing out from constant use. It was necessary and prudent to incorporate the congregation as well as the larger community in the campaign.

However, we caution that if you do go outside of a church, your campaign is probably going to take longer because you will have to execute an organization and communication plan above and beyond the membership of the congregation. It may take longer, it may take more in terms of management time and oversight, but the financial rewards usually are there.

Also, other types of persons besides church members might help in your campaign. There may be extended families who have relatives buried in the church cemetery, and whose descendants might wish to participate. There may be a sentimental attachment to a church by someone who attended as a youth but has not been back for some period of time. There are members of what we might euphemistically call the "Church Alumni Society" that should be researched and approached.

Do not neglect to overturn all the stones possible. If other groups are using your building during the day or evening, you might approach these groups and ask for gifts, especially groups like AA or any other self-help groups that use the building on a regular basis.

Some older churches are on a State or National Register of Historical Places. There may be the possibility of government grants at the local, state, or federal levels to assist in maintaining physical structures, especially if the program has to do with physical restoration or historic preservation. Generally, these governmental bodies cannot assist any type of program that has to do with Christian education and worship. But they might be able to help you preserve the facade or integrity of the building. This is especially true in some of our larger cities where you may find an urban foundation or a local governmental unit that can be helpful.

Also, there are some foundations throughout the United States that can assist in historic preservation of sacred spaces. Do look into this, but do not hold your breath because these gifts are difficult to obtain. It may be worth looking into if you are trying to preserve an historical structure. In one recent campaign, a church served as a national monument. Friends and groups outside of the congregation were encouraged to assist in the preservation of the building. The church was able to present itself to a larger public as a monument, eligible for corporate gifts and worthy of support from friends who would not normally give to church campaigns. So explore these options, but for a suburban church, a church in a smaller town, or a church that does not have any type of community service that is of an outstanding nature, it is best to count on support only from those within the congregation.

What to Expect of the Congregation?

First, how do we define the membership of a church? This can vary from church to church, denomination to denomination. Generally speaking, the people on your mailing list comprise the membership. These are the people who receive the questionnaire mailed during the feasibility study. This is the body from which you hope to draw the majority of your financial strength during your campaign.

The stark reality is that for most churches in most mainline denominations, only 50% to 70% of the family units who are called members are giving regularly to a church either through a formal pledge or with regular contributions. Even though one may communicate regularly with the other 50%, 40% or 30% of the church "membership," it is usually very difficult to involve them in a capital program.

One rough rule is, "If people are not giving regularly to the annual budget to support the ongoing ministry of the church, do not expect them to give to the campaign itself." This is very frustrating to clergy or lay committee chairs who know that certain "members" may be owners of large businesses or have considerable wealth that could help to underwrite the church campaign but choose not to. Generally, the only time campaigns have been successful with extremely wealthy people, who do not give regularly to the church but are claimed as members, is when a financial peer calls on them and says to the effect, "I gave to your museum campaign (or whatever) last year. Can you join me in giving to our church?"

This is disappointing, but it does not mean that these individuals are not generous. They may be financially generous throughout the community but not to or through the church.

With appreciation to The Rev. Hugh Magers, the former Director of Stewardship for the Domestic and Foreign Missionary Society of The Episcopal Church, and drawing on our own experience, we would like to help you visualize the categories of people who normally give regularly to the church. While we hesitate to divide people into categories, and we recognize that situations overlap, the following may be useful to your understanding of your congregation.

GIVING PROFILE OF A CONGREGATION

Percentage of congregation	Who	Giving
10%–20%	The Converted	Generous donors or tithers or those working toward the tithe.
35%–55%	The Committed	1%–3% of their income
30%–40%	The Uncommitted	Little or nothing

The Converted

Denominations vary and churches within the denominations differ, but among the membership are people whom we shall call "The Converted." They represent the 10% to 20% of the members who try to tithe or are tithing. They are extremely faithful and when they make a gift, they are not giving to the church, they are "giving to God." Most are on a spiritual journey and will be very supportive, to the extent that they can, of a capital campaign. However, many of these people are already "tapped out" because they are so generous on an annual basis.

The Committed

The next group of individuals is called the "Committed." These are people who compose anywhere from 35% to 55% of the congregation. These folk give but they generally do not tithe. They willingly serve on leadership committees, and they attend church regularly. They are on a journey, but not yet totally "converted." They are giving, not necessarily to God, but to the church.

They can be demanding in what they expect of the church in terms of services. They want a Christian education program for the children, the sermon to be well-prepared, and the facilities to be adequate and clean, especially the restrooms. For their financial generosity, they expect value. If the church fails to deliver service or if there is conflict among top leadership, these individuals often go shopping for another church.

There is a great deal less loyalty to denominations than there has been in previous generations. The "committed" individuals are quicker to move from denomination to denomination in order to find a comfort level and value for their giving.

Yet these individuals are absolutely critical to a capital campaign. This is one reason to conduct extensive readiness activities, to carry out a feasibility study, and to prepare a campaign brochure, because many of these people have a high need for information. They want to be involved in the decision-making process. Leave these people out of the decision-making process and their giving will be extremely low. This group is composed of many opinion makers and many very busy people. They want to spend their time wisely, and to make sure that their donations are thoughtfully used.

The Uncommitted

The third group are the ones called the "Uncommitted." These individuals may compose anywhere from 30% to 40% of the congregation. They are on the rolls, they receive the newsletter, but they do not attend services very often, maybe on Christmas or Easter, or perhaps for marriages and funerals. They do not give very much, if at all. These folks are uncommitted, and rather than giving one percent to three percent of their income or even considering tithing, they give nothing or they merely "tip." This group may contain some extremely wealthy people who have no regular pattern of giving their support to the church, and yet they call themselves members of the congregation. Enlisting their help in any capital campaign more often than not is usually frustrating and disappointing.

The Length of a Campaign

How long does a church campaign last? One model indicates anywhere from three to five months, depending upon the size of the goal and congregation. Three to five months may be required for the act of solicitation, but it may take several months for a feasibility study. You may spend several months, even years, in the Readiness Phase just to prepare for the feasibility study.

The involvement of financial leadership, the season of the year, the need for increased public relations within the congregation, the informing of major gift prospects, and the size of the goal are determining factors (factors usually revealed in the feasibility study) on the length of the campaign. We do not recommend that you rush through the campaign. Many contributions are often missed in a compressed effort. Leadership gifts may be smaller than they should have been because of the failure adequately to inform and enthusiastically involve all prospects.

The Campaign Season

What is the best time of the year to do the campaign? Traditionally, campaigns have been held September to June. However, recent experience indicates that it is sometimes possible to hold campaigns during the summer. It may take a little bit longer because more people are on vacation, but it is not always a bad time of the year. The kick-off event can actually become a 4th of July picnic or some kind of outdoor activity.

American life is extremely busy, and there is no perfect time of the year anymore. Tax advantages are usually not what encourages one to give to a church capital campaign.

The Capital Drive and Annual Stewardship

The question is asked, "Can one conduct a capital campaign at the same time as the annual stewardship drive?" Many would say "no." The realistic answer is "yes."

Remember, we talked about church members being busy. What a wonderful opportunity to hold up the ministry of the church by asking people to contribute 1) to the annual stewardship drive and 2) to the capital campaign.

Now, if it is a matter of members saying, "I cannot give to both," then do not push for the capital gift. The annual stewardship effort must come first. If one cannot give to both, they do not give to the capital program. The feasibility study usually will ask the question about both being accomplished at the same time. This puts people on alert. If workers are trained properly and if a communication plan is executed, a church can accomplish both activities at the same time. Volunteers will appreciate the savings in time. Given a choice, invest time in ministry, not in raising funds for ministry.

Our experience has been that annual stewardship can actually increase during a capital drive. The workers are trained, organized, and encouraged to make those important one-on-one calls.

Building Endowment

Can gifts for the endowment be raised at the same time as funds for brick and mortar? The answer is "yes." Many campaigns have some combination of raising money for restoration and raising money for endowment.

The question is asked, "How to raise endowment?" First, by asking directly for pledges over a multi-year period. Second, by engaging in a planned giving program as part of your process.

Can a church conduct a planned giving program and endowment drive at the same time as a brick and mortar capital campaign? "Yes," we have been successful at doing all of these. As long as people are focused on the ministry of the church, why not use all the tools that are available? On a number of occasions, even during the feasibility study process, we have identified and helped create planned gifts, such as charitable remainder trusts or real estate donations.

We hasten to add, however, that the endowment effort, begun as part of focused attention during your capital drive, is merely the beginning. A planned giving program should be held quarterly, year after year, to encourage people to remember the church in their estate plans. If done properly, a church can have a successful capital drive, a successful annual stewardship effort, and make a significant beginning in building endowment!

However, raising money in a capital campaign is a little like playing a hand of bridge. Whether one is bidding 6 no-trump or 2 diamonds, it is going to take the same thoughtful effort! The same with a capital program; certain activities have to occur no matter the size of the goal. Generally speaking, the larger the goal, the less expensive it is on a percentage basis to provide the management oversight and communications necessary to achieve the level of success you would like to have.

A Sample Budget

The sample budget for your campaign should include the following items:

1. Feasibility study costs.

2. The management fee to the firm that is providing the service for your campaign to include travel, meals, and lodging for the campaign manager. Be wary of firms that charge a percentage of the goal achieved. Such can encourage "high pressure" tactics and dubious gift reporting.

3. Clerical support.

4. Appropriate computer software to record and track gifts, produce letters, mailing labels, and financial reports.

5. Office equipment which includes a computer, printer, copier, fax, and answering machine.

6. Office supplies.

7. Meal meetings.

8. Kick-off event.

9. Telephone.

10. Campaign materials—brochures, pledge cards, etc.

11. Postage.

12. Contingencies.

13. Campaign video, if desired.

14. Honorariums, plaques, etc.

This is usually the financial structure necessary to accomplish what you are doing.

Do You Need Capital Campaign Counsel?

Regardless of the size of your goal, you may wish to consider contracting with a campaign management firm that has conducted church capital drives. Even relatively small campaigns can benefit from outside counsel, at least for the preparation of a fund raising plan which would include a time line, job descriptions for the tasks of leadership, worker orientation and training, and the production of brochures and materials necessary for the success of the effort.

The level of appropriate management oversight needed varies from church to church depending on the availability of leadership, the complexity of the project, and the size of the goal and congregation.

What to Expect from Outside Counsel?

Your outside counsel can be thought of as the producer or director of a play, a drama in which the volunteers are the main actors. The preparation necessary to put on a play is done by your campaign counsel. Do not expect your counsel to solicit gifts; this rarely happens. The solicitation of gifts is a one-on-one activity conducted by volunteers, clergy leadership, and financial peers.

Remember, a financial peer almost always solicits a financial peer. A person capable of giving $1,000 calls on someone else capable of giving $1,000. The $100 donor does not ask someone for a $1,000 donation.

Do expect counsel to do the following:

1. Organize your campaign calendar.

2. Create job descriptions for leadership.

3. Assist in identifying and evaluating advance gift prospects.

4. Coordinate the writing and production of materials.

5. Assist planning for events such as kick-off dinners and Celebration Sundays.

6. Provide orientation, ongoing training, and leadership.

7. Ensure that the communications plan is being executed.

8. Provide both strategic and tactical advice.

9. Ensure gifts are properly recorded and acknowledged.

Outside counsel will set deadlines for you, force you to do the appropriate evaluations, and ensure, to the greatest extent possible, that you will do one-on-one calls. In short, your counsel provides the game plan and discipline to ensure success.

There are some other reasons to consider outside counsel. Number one, you are hiring time. There is a word that describes Americans, and that word is "over-scheduled." Yet what is required is time to manage the complex task of going from zero revenue to several hundred thousand, perhaps several million dollars, in a relatively short period of time. Someone has to write and execute the plan, see that deadlines are met, and manage the office to make sure appropriate communication occurs. When you bring in outside counsel, you can be assured that those activities are going to be carried out as effectively and efficiently as possible.

Of course, you are also hiring expertise. You are bringing in someone who is trained and has the experience to execute a methodology that has worked well in church after church after church. There are certain methodologies that have proven very effective. Some consulting firms stress certain nuances; other firms emphasize other techniques. Basically, however, the process involves getting people organized, sharing information, and executing the plan.

Check to be sure that the person you bring in has all the organizational people skills necessary to take the project from A to Z in a short period of time. "Fund raising" conjures all sorts of concepts. There is nothing mysterious about it; it is working with a management and communication plan. It takes time, involves many people, and requires a great deal of information sharing. What you should expect when you bring in someone from the outside is that all the nuts and bolts are put in place and that nothing is going to fall through the cracks. The investment you make in outside management, for whatever period of time, will help you to have a much more efficient and effective campaign. If you try to do it yourself, you may find yourself not ready for meetings or not being as efficient in encouraging people to maximize their giving potential. You may lack the discipline to see that the cards are worked so that the campaign will end on time. Volunteers do not have the commitment to each other that they have to paid expertise!

The question is asked, "If we use an outside consulting firm, how much does it cost?" Fees vary depending on the service time, the expertise, the location of the firm, and your location. Generally speaking, daily fees are about the same you would pay an attorney, a CPA, or other professional advisor. However, there may be travel costs associated with the fee, either on top of it or included in it. Be sure you have a written understanding.

How much outside consulting service is necessary? Only the service necessary to accomplish your task. Again this varies. Some firms place a manager on site continuously for a number of weeks over a number of months. Others promote in and out service, limiting the days of consulting. In a time of fax machines and E-mail, it is not necessary to be on-site as often as one used to. Thanks to airplanes, no church, church school, or agency is more than a few hours away from your consultant. For smaller campaigns, a mentoring relationship with the church can be established.

CHAPTER SIX

How to Prepare for a Capital Campaign for a Regional Church Body

"Where there is no vision the people perish." Proverbs 29:18

IN THIS CHAPTER, WE ARE GOING TO EXPLORE THE DYNAMICS REQUIRED TO develop a successful effort that involves many individual churches.

Often there is a need for an annual giving, capital or endowment effort for church agencies, charities, camps, college chaplaincies, seminaries, or judicatory bodies such as dioceses, synods, conferences or districts.

For the sake of simplicity, let us examine the preparation necessary for a campaign often run in the Episcopal Church—the diocesan capital campaign. The lessons provided and the methodology described are similar to all extensive regional and national denominational efforts.

The Diocesan Campaign

Conducting a diocesan wide capital campaign is a time-consuming, risk-taking effort for the bishop and diocesan leadership. It is not to be taken lightly. Much prayer, soul-searching, visioning, and communication must occur if a bishop is to lead a diocese in a successful effort.

Just as in a church campaign, diocesan leadership should consider a capital drive effort in three major phases:

1. The Readiness Process

2. The Feasibility Study

3. The Campaign

In the first recorded church capital campaign (remember Exodus, Chapters 35 and 36), it was easy (or so it seems by hindsight) for Moses to know the will of God. God challenged Moses and Aaron to build a tabernacle in the wilderness. People gave so joyfully that Moses had to command the donors to quit giving! This is the first successful church campaign, and probably the last, where leadership had to tell people NOT to give more! (Exodus, 36:5-7)

Discerning the will of God is not as easy for most modern-day bishops as it was for Moses. Leadership may have a vision of enhanced ministry that requires financial resources to implement that goal. For most dioceses and church agencies, communicating the vision and seeking to know the will of the Almighty is a process and not an instant revelation. Every diocese must involve lay and clergy in the visioning and discernment process. Too frequently, the leadership has had to stop in the middle of a campaign to explain the purposes and goals of the diocesan fund drive.

The Readiness Program

As we have noted, people support and contribute more readily to causes when they are involved in the creation of the case statement (the reasons for the campaign). This is true of clergy as well as laity. Both must prayerfully discern for themselves what God is calling the church and people to accomplish.

And, of course, if people are not aware a campaign is going to occur, they cannot plan to give to it. As advocated in an earlier chapter, communicate, communicate, communicate, and then communicate again.

It is normal for local clergy and laity to feel financially threatened when the diocese or some church charity or school considers raising funds either by directly approaching members of the congregation or through local churches. However, sharing the vision and explaining how the campaign would unfold helps to reduce anxiety, encourages cooperation, and can produce early thoughts of gifting.

Clergy and laity need to be reminded that many church members are giving generously to local community capital campaigns. Yet, despite that fact, many members will respond to a diocesan vision if an urgent and compelling cause is shared with them. A diocesan-wide campaign does not reduce the annual giving potential of a congregation; eventually the opposite occurs. People become comfortable with giving at higher levels and often pass this generosity along in future years to the local church.

By involving church leaders early in the planning process, many begin to think about their own local needs. This is especially true in a diocesan campaign. A sizeable percentage of churches will elect to embark on their own campaigns during the diocesan effort. In part this occurs because the diocese dared to share a vision, set a calendar, and enforce deadlines. Such a local endeavor, while somewhat reducing the potential for diocesan gifts, does develop financial resources for other vital ministries.

If planned giving is to be a part of a diocesan effort to build endowment, consider inviting churches to join in establishing a common goal for planned giving (wills, charitable trusts, real estate, and other gifts) at the local level. Leadership might ask churches to join in a Partnership for Ministry Resource Development. Local leadership is more likely to embrace the proposed campaign with enthusiasm if they perceive that the diocese is reaching out to help all parts of the church in financial development and if their local congregation will also benefit from the effort.

Naturally, by carrying out readiness activities, the eventual feasibility study will reveal more enthusiasm, higher possible gift levels, additional names of leadership, and more cooperation from clergy and lay leaders. This increases the potential success of a campaign.

How Readiness Activities are Conducted for a Diocesan Campaign

Organizing and communicating in a geographical area the size of a diocese, with numerous churches, is always a challenge.

Here is a step-by-step method to engage leadership and provide both clergy and lay people alike with a vision for ministry.

- Generally, a bishop and a few diocesan leaders begin to perceive the need for funds for enhanced ministries in the diocese. Usually these thoughts are shared first with diocesan council or the diocesan executive committee. The council may appoint a "Visioning Committee" or an "Exploratory Capital Campaign Committee." The appointment of a committee should be announced in diocesan publications.

- The Exploratory Committee should draft the first statement of possible projects to be funded.

- The bishop and other diocesan leaders, both clergy and lay, should begin preaching the vision, asking for prayers and feedback.

- The leadership should then organize a clergy and lay conference, break into small groups, study the vision, and report back to a facilitator. A consultant can explain in detail how a diocesan campaign would work.

■ The bishop would ask faithful people to pray about what they may be called to do in response to the considered vision, and in response to their own calling to preach the Gospel and build the church. The clergy should be encouraged to inform their leadership and congregations, and begin to explore locally what is required of the community of faith and what a response to the calling should be.

■ The revised vision should be taken to area meetings where it can be shared with clergy, members of diocesan committees, congregational leaders and delegates to the next diocesan convention. Feedback is encouraged. Leadership might challenge the churches to consider a possible "Partnership in Ministry" participation. Begin and end these sessions with scripture and prayer. This is a true search for the voice of God.

■ The outcome of all these activities should be reported in the diocesan newspaper and any in-house newsletters to clergy and lay leaders.

■ The bishop, clergy and lay leadership should meet as many local church leaders and major donor prospects as possible. Begin searching for top financial leadership, both clergy and lay, to lead the campaign. God uses the abundance of wealthy people to build the church and enable ministry. Do not be bashful when involving wealthy people in this cause. They too need to be encouraged to give and lead through the spiritual interaction that comes from conversation and challenge by a bishop or clergy person.

■ At some point, the vision is refined by the Exploratory Committee and returned to the diocesan council. Following endorsement, it is presented at the diocesan convention, where all congregations are represented. Each part of the proposed program should be thoroughly examined during the convention, often in committee. Give people the opportunity to ask questions. Let members be challenged to pray, study, and reason together, both discerning and visioning.

From this convention, may come a resolution to conduct a feasibility study. At this juncture, an outside consulting firm is usually employed to prepare an objective evaluation; a survey will take several months. The bishop and council may be authorized to launch a campaign if the study is positive. Or, the convention may ask for a specially-called session to study the results of the survey and vote whether or not to proceed.

Throughout this process continue to share information. Remember, every member of the church is continuously asked to give to many worthy causes. A diocesan campaign may be a "holy endeavor," but it too requires the use of every communication skill and organizational methodology available.

Why a Feasibility Study?

The bishop and leadership may have a vision and believe that they are responding to God's will. There also comes a time when they must know the will of the clergy and lay leadership. That formal survey to explore the feelings of the diocese is known as the feasibility study.

A diocesan feasibility study seeks to ascertain the following:

- Do clergy and laity support the proposed projects?
- Which projects have priority?
- What projects omitted from the proposed plans should be included?
- Are clergy and laity willing to volunteer their time?
- Are they willing to make gifts?
- Do sizeable leadership gifts exist?
- Are new leadership gift prospects suggested?
- Would people consider planned giving?
- Can the projected financial goal be attained?
- What financial goal is appropriate?
- Which churches are considering their own capital campaigns?
- Are there conflicting community and church agency capital campaigns?
- Is the suggested timing right?
- Will the economy support a campaign at the suggested time?
- Generally speaking, are clergy and laity in favor of a capital drive?

A formal study may take two to four months to complete. Materials have to be prepared; people must be interviewed and others must receive a mail questionnaire. All clergy and lay leaders (diocesan and local) should express their opinion formally. Leadership gift prospects should be seen or surveyed.

A study does not commit a diocese to a campaign. The survey may suggest delay or revision of the goal and/or may encourage a campaign along the lines of the suggested goal. It also allows the diocese to work closely with the selected consulting firm to determine if the company performs appropriately and if the chemistry is good between the leadership and the consultants.

After the Study, Share the News

Assuming the study is positive, it is now time to prepare for the campaign. Share the results of the study with the diocese through newspapers, newsletters, the spoken word, clergy conferences, council and convention meetings, and key leadership meetings.

Diocesan convention, either before or after the study, must vote to proceed or not. Use this occasion to celebrate the expected increase in mission and ministry. Prepare to share the Good News of God in Christ, and the opportunity to go forth with enthusiasm to encourage others to give to enhance the church and its mission.

The Diocesan Campaign

And finally, recruit leadership, communicate, organize, and ask people to join in giving. By asking, people are offered the gift of information, and the gift of changing the world and enhancing ministry through a donation.

Based on geography, the size of the diocese, and readiness of all churches to participate, a campaign may take six to eighteen months. The bishop, clergy and lay leadership must set aside time for communication and for the asking of gifts.

Usually leadership will divide a diocesan campaign into two major divisions. A quiet advance gifts phase in which major donor prospects will be informed and visited asking for their financial participation. Diocesan leadership works very closely with local parishes during this phase to ensure cooperation.

After the advance gifts phase, and with a considerable portion of the pledges and donations in hand, diocesan leadership will officially kick off the campaign with a central event, such as a diocesan-wide dinner, and proclaim a Dedication Sunday throughout the diocese. During this second or Congregational Phase, workers in local churches will call on their fellow members to join in giving to the diocesan effort.

During these months, it is not business as usual, but rather the wonderful opportunity to harvest gifts for ministry. Without resources, the church is less than it can be. With resources, the Gospel of Jesus Christ can be more fully shared with a world in desperate need of the hope and grace of our Creator. Go forth to love and serve the Lord!

CHAPTER SEVEN

How to Get Ready for a Church School Capital Campaign

To this point, we have examined how to prepare and conduct congregational and regional church body campaigns. Let us now examine a church school capital drive. By church school, we mean a school independent of government ownership, attached to and/or formally sponsored by a congregation or denomination. The number of church schools has grown significantly in recent decades in the United States. While financially underwritten by tuition, few schools could survive without annual giving support from the church sponsor, parents, friends, alumni, and grandparents of students. In this chapter, we examine how to prepare for a capital drive.

As with a church or denominational capital campaign, positioning a church school for a capital drive is as important as conducting the funds drive itself. To maximize your school's potential for soliciting and receiving needed financial resources, carefully consider the following steps as the part of the Readiness Phase:

1. Identify the needs of the school.

2. Identify the constituency.

3. Communicate the needs.

Remember the points on the "wheel of fortune" in Chapter 2. Let us examine these points one by one.

Identify the Needs of the School

Why is the school leadership considering a capital improvement program? Do you need to expand by adding a chapel, classrooms, a lunch room, library, laboratories, or gymnasium? Is the school in need of remodeling or considerable maintenance? Is the physical plant suffering from deficiencies?

Appoint a building committee to meet with an architect or contractor. Invite them to tour the facilities and make recommendations. Teachers or staff who use or will use the facilities should also be involved. Their input is valuable. Consider appointing senior students, parents and grandparents of students, alumni, and influential or helpful members of the community to this committee. In addition to bringing fresh ideas to the process, these members will help to interpret the project to the constituencies they represent. Visit other schools and examine how they have handled space needs.

For the church-related school, one must always work closely with the clergy and official leadership of the church. A church school may need formal church approval before engaging in a campaign. Follow the guidelines, either formal or informal, appropriate to your situation. Appoint church representatives to serve as liaisons to your planning committee.

Your architect is a critical part of the team. Is she or he experienced in school design? It is important to discuss fees in advance and to describe your vision as completely as possible.

Working with an architect, your building committee should prepare and present first plans to the board. After reviewing the plans, it may be time to broadcast this vision to the school's constituencies. This leads to our next major point on the "wheel of fortune."

Identify the Constituency

Who will make the gifts that are essential to ensure the success of your capital drive? Ideally, your school should already have a strong annual giving program that benefits from the on-going support of parents of current students, your board, and alumni.

Also consider these sources:

■ grandparents and other relatives of students

■ parents of former students

■ members of the sponsoring church

■ the larger local community (sometimes called "friends of the school")

■ local philanthropists known to support education

■ foundations, corporations, and businesses.

Communicate the Needs

Neglecting to increase awareness of the value of your school, its programs, and the proposed project is to court failure. You must regularly share information on your plans with the groups listed above. Devise a communication plan for each group. Plans may include the following:

- newsletters

- bulletins to parents

- bulletin inserts (for the church)

- alumni magazines

- open house

- group tours

- private in-home meetings

- parents' day/night

- grandparents' day

- chamber of commerce sponsored events

- stories and announcements in the media

- luncheons

- lobby displays

- speeches to local civic groups

- regular reports to your sponsoring church and religious denomination.

Tell your story in as many ways as possible and as often as possible. A strong public relations program will not only attract financial support but also new students.

Conduct a Feasibility Study

At the appropriate time, a key part of your communication is the feasibility study. An outside consultant or firm should systematically survey your constituencies to answer such fundamental questions as these:

1. Are your constituents supportive of the project?

2. Is the proposed campaign timing appropriate?

3. Are leadership gifts available?

4. Can the proposed financial goal be attained?

5. Is leadership available and willing to serve?

6. Is the sponsoring church supportive?

This study provides critical research necessary before launching your effort. You may find that you have to downsize your project if it is too ambitious for the financial potential of your prospects. Or you may be forced to postpone the project if the timing is wrong (for example, competing campaigns or a weak economy).

If the data is positive, you can now report back to the board and sponsoring church with the study, fine tune your financial plans, including any necessary borrowing, and move forward with confidence because of the following:

1. You correctly identified and responded to your school's needs.

2. You identified the individuals and groups necessary for the financial success of this effort.

3. You fully informed these individuals about your school and plans. Furthermore, you have formally sought their opinions about the project and have acted on that information (perhaps modifying financial goals, plans, or timing).

If you have thoughtfully and carefully engaged in the above "readiness" activities, than enthusiastically launch your campaign and prepare to be of greater service to your students, the community, and the church you serve.

Some Observations

For this chapter, the key word is "church." One, because it identifies the uniqueness of the school. Two, because more often than not the church and school conduct the campaign together! Many times both institutions share facilities and are seeking to increase and improve physical space. Third, the participation of church members and their willingness to give is critical. Often parents of school children are young and lack the ability to make major gifts. Without the participation of the sponsoring church, the gift total may be minimal.

The Church School Campaign

As we have discussed in previous chapters for both the church and area-wide church capital campaigns, divide your school campaign into these phases:

- Organiztion.

- Leadership recruitment.

- Advance Gifts.

- Smaller Gifts.

- Acknowledgment of gifts and leadership.

A church school normally has a larger, more diverse constituency than a church. The campaign may take longer and require more organization because more groups have to be coordinated and communicated with. If there is a significant alumni group, travel may be involved, again lengthening the campaign but providing more prospects for donations.

CHAPTER EIGHT

How to Prepare for a Church Agency Capital Campaign

MOST CHURCH AGENCIES OR CHARITIES UNDERTAKE CAPITAL CAMPAIGNS ONLY once every five or ten years. Planning and preparation alone can take months, or even years, and involve dozens of people.

Remember these basic principles (regardless of the type of capital campaign):

1. People give to people. The most effective way to solicit a pledge is through committed individuals visiting peers and stating, "I believe in this cause. I am supporting it financially and personally. Will you join me in considering a gift?"

2. People give to urgent and compelling causes. They do not give to causes that seem unimportant to them, that are poorly planned or managed, or that are ineffectively communicated.

3. People more often donate time and money to campaigns when they have been invited to provide input and advice. Volunteers and prospective donors should feel that they have ownership of a campaign. People best support campaigns when they have the opportunity to participate in the decision making process.

The following steps explore the fundamental "Readiness" activities necessary to help position a church agency to launch a successful capital campaign. These steps, of course, may be modified depending upon your organization's particular situation.

Assess Your Level of Readiness

None of us would build a house without drawing plans and laying a sure foundation. The same principles are true for any capital campaign.

Study closely the following matrix that is designed to examine your organization's current state of readiness and provide specific goals to work toward. Honestly examine your agency's readiness posture, and be prepared to address concerns.

Is Your Church Agency Ready for a Capital Campaign?

by Susan Stuart
Vice President, Holliman Associates

The items in each section, if read in sequence from top to bottom, will help you to determine if:

1. **you are ready to undertake a campaign;**
2. **you could be ready with more preparation;**
3. **you should consider delaying your campaign.**

The Need

1. The organization has identified specific and urgent needs.
2. The organization is in the process of identifying specific and urgent needs.
3. The organization must still come to consensus on priority needs.

The Case

1. The organization has developed and written a compelling case explaining the campaign goals.
2. The organization is developing a compelling case.
3. The organization has not developed a compelling case.

The Board

1. The Board of Directors understands and embraces the long-term commitment of time and resources required for a successful campaign and recognizes that fund raising is not only their responsibility, but a top priority.
2. The Board of Directors is willing to learn more about the personal commitment and financial investment required as well as how to solicit gifts from their peers.
3. The Board of Directors has a limited ability to make commit-

ments, provide leadership, or is still working to overcome its
discomfort with solicitation and/or making financial donations.

Relationships

1. Board members and key volunteers have existing peer relationships with philanthropic leaders, church leaders and
major donors.

2. Board members and key volunteers have access to philanthropic leaders, major donors and major gift prospects.

3. There are few or no relationships with church, philanthropic
and community leaders.

Communication

1. The organization communicates often (more than five times a
year) with its donors, constituents and prospects using newsletters and other public relations tools.

2. The organization communicates occasionally (two to four
times per year) with its donor base by newsletters, group meetings, occasional visits, church talks, and through media outlets.

3. The organization does not have a public relations plan and
communicates infrequently with its constituency.

The Budget

1. The project budget is as accurate as it possibly can be at this
point in the planning process.

2. The project budget is an estimate provided by professionals.

3. The project requires more accurate financial projections before
sharing a budget.

Leadership

1. Articulate, enthusiastic individuals are available to lead and to
share the vision.

2. Articulate, enthusiastic individuals are available on a limited
basis.

3. No one is available to lead, make decisions or share the vision with the community.

The Staff

1. The staff understands and supports the need for a campaign.
2. The staff is being educated about the need for a campaign.
3. The staff is not aware that a campaign is being considered.

The Community

1. All other funding opportunities have been examined before turning to the church denomination and community at large for support.
2. Other funding opportunities are being explored.
3. Sources of financial support are not aware of the organization's needs.

Remember that it is imperative to communicate with potential donors and to build a base of philanthropic leadership. Failure to do so will delay your campaign and reduce your potential to receive gifts.

Preparing for a capital campaign may also provide an opportunity to conduct an organizational self-assessment. Your organization may benefit from an evaluation of its governance, planning, marketing, fiscal management, personnel management, and other aspects of internal and external operations including its relationship to sponsoring churches. Examining an organization's strengths and weaknesses in these areas educates those involved in the process and may reveal opportunities to better position the organization for future challenges.

As with most capital drives, the most common reasons for conducting a campaign are to build a new building or remodel an existing one, although an extraordinary leap in programming and endowment may also inspire a campaign.

Your Board of Directors will appoint a committee, sometimes called a Needs Assessment Committee to articulate how a campaign will enable the organization to better serve its mission. Most often, this takes the form of evaluating current and future needs, considering challenges and opportunities, and formalizing a case statement.

The organization's leadership should establish preliminary and final report dates and a written outline of the information required. Since the report will include recommendations for strategic action, include volunteers with a sense of vision and mission in this group.

Make sure you set aside an appropriate block of time for meetings with the Board to allow for full discussion, and, if needed, revision of the plan.

If your community has a Capital Campaign Review Board, be sure to educate them about potential projects and ask about reporting and scheduling guidelines. If your agency receives United Way funding, you may also need the approval of their campaign review board before launching a campaign. Of course, being church related, the sponsoring church, churches, or denomination may need to give their permission and/or endorsement.

Create A Framework to Support the Project

Once the Board has voted on the report of the Needs Assessment Committee, it is time to define the project in more detail. In a capital project, several task forces should be created to act simultaneously. Work may include: screening architects and builders, working with bankers about financing options, meeting with real estate agents, interviewing professional fund raising counsel, and developing a preliminary budget.

Your organization's size and tradition will determine how best to delegate these responsibilities. Be sure that the individuals or committees assigned to study options and deal with issues clearly understand the tasks they are being asked to complete. Again, remember the importance of setting deadlines.

Share the News and Invite Input

Once you select an architect, it makes good sense to commission a draft plan with estimated costs for approval by your leadership. Share the building plans with as many of your constituents as possible. Print newsletter articles and hold cottage meetings and receptions to invite feedback. If the proposed project is sizeable, consider constructing and displaying a model in appropriate places. Pay special attention to potential major donors. By all means, keep the sponsoring church or denomination involved and informed every step of the way.

Find creative ways to continuously inform and involve your organization's key volunteers, staff, and constituents. Liberally delegate tasks to as many people as possible. While this may take some extra time, the benefits of sharing your enthusiasm for the project, asking for assistance, and including many people in the process should more than compensate.

Don't overlook a thoughtful, well-timed public relations effort. You can begin with low-key information sharing and build to coincide with major capital campaign activities. Remember that most organizations do not communicate enough with their prospective donors.

Authorize a Feasibility Study

As with the church, area-wide church or church school campaign, the agency's financial potential usually cannot be determined accurately without a thorough feasibility study. Personal interviews with key leadership and potential major donors as well as a mail survey to your constituency should occur.

This two-track approach informs a large number of supporters about the organization's intentions, helps to establish an achievable financial goal for the campaign, and invites feedback and involvement.

Once completed, a good feasibility study will answer the following questions for a church agency:

1. Are the organization's key volunteers and major donors supportive of the plans as proposed?

2. Will the larger civic and philanthropic community support a campaign?

3. Is the sponsoring church and denomination supportive?

4. What are the priorities as seen by the general constituency?

5. Are people willing to give to the proposed capital campaign?

6. If so, what potential leadership gifts are available?

7. Is the financial goal attainable, or does it need to be modified?

8. What is the best time for a campaign?

9. What additional information should be shared?

10. Who should chair the campaign and who should serve on the various committees?

11. Can the organization raise funds through planned gifts such as bequests in wills, gifts of appreciated stock, real estate, charitable trusts, and/or life insurance, or in-kind gifts?

As noted in earlier chapters, a feasibility study helps to clarify the vision that will become the focal point of the campaign. It can uncover concerns or problems and identify campaign volunteers. It is a vital investment in the success of any future capital drive effort.

Leadership Makes Campaign Decisions

If the feasibility study is positive, the Board of Directors and key volunteer leaders should make the final decision on the size, scope, and timing of the campaign. Sometimes, the dream is too ambitious and plans must be revised. It will take time to review and decide how to fine tune the plans and financial objectives. This process must occur before launching your drive.

Final Thoughts Before the Campaign

The unique challenges of a campaign can spark fresh opportunities to fulfill the mission, make friends for the organization, and renew the dedication and spirit of current volunteers and staff. As with any process, there are peaks and valleys . However, with proper planning, wise execution, a strong commitment to attracting and involving philanthropic and church leadership, and an urgent and compelling case, you will achieve success.

CHAPTER NINE

What to Expect from Your Church Architect

by Kenneth M. Graves, AIA

WE HAVE ASKED OUR COLLEAGUE, KENNETH M. GRAVES, AN ARCHITECT FROM SAN Antonio, Texas, to write this chapter. Ken has assisted churches, schools, businesses and individuals in planning wisely for new construction. In addition to being a fine architect, he is a dedicated Christian, having served in numerous leadership capacities in his local church. Although this chapter revolves around church construction, the steps outlined apply to any church school or church agency.

Consider the following: a good architect and proper planning can go a long way toward ensuring that any construction or restoration will best serve the ministries of your church, school, or agency.

Before you turn a spadeful of dirt or hammer a nail, ask yourself if your church has the following:

1. A building committee—The group that should represent a cross section of all interested parties, the official church leadership, the staff, committee chair persons, and all age groups. (Don't forget to include those with construction and/or engineering experience.) This committee should communicate with the rest of the congregation throughout the entire planning process. Gaps in communication can cause problems further into the program.

2. The master plan—A comprehensive written plan created by your architect that reflects your vision.

3. A realistic budget—A financial outline that articulates what is achievable through fund raising and borrowing to complete your vision. It is important to have a vision, but the vision must coincide with financial reality. How much is in your building fund? How much can or do you wish to raise from a capital campaign and/or borrowing?

The Need for an Architect

An architect can be compared to the conductor of a symphony orchestra. It is the conductor who coordinates the musicians and brings their individual talents together to produce harmonious music. Like a conductor, an architect is trained to be the overall director for the myriad of disciplines that go into planning and constructing a building. It is his/her expertise that will pull all individuals into the cohesive team that will work toward your project's completion.

The architect also works with many other professionals as a team. These professionals will produce required documents and plans. An architect is licensed by your state and places his/her name and State Registration Seal on all documents that are produced so he/she is ultimately responsible for the plans. Depending on the size and complexity of your project, other professionals involved may include a civil engineer, structural engineer, mechanical engineer, electrical engineer, plumbing engineer, interior designer, and/or landscape architect.

How to Find an Architect

Interview architects who are recommended to you and who have experience in church design. If the architect is already familiar with liturgical language, you will spend less time explaining the meaning of terms and theological symbolism. Also, the architect should know from experience what spaces are required and how large they need to be. Ask other churches for recommendations or talk to friends who have worked with architects.

Invite each recommended architect to submit a statement of interest to your committee. This is normal procedure and provides you with a detailed résumé outlining work experience. From these submittals, you can develop a list of architects to invite for an interview.

Selecting an Architect

The interview will tell you how well your personalities are going to work together. Pick an architect that your committee is comfortable with since you will be working closely with this person for a number of months and relying on his/her judgment. Request references and follow through.

Hire an architect only after your leadership has agreed on the following:

■ The personalities will work well together.

■ You have confidence in his/her advice and will accept it based on his/her experience.

■ You have verified through previous clients that the architect comes to you well recommended.

■ You understand what he/she will be doing and how much it will cost to develop your plans.

Fees

During the interview process, it is important to discuss the hourly fee or compensation arrangements. Architects often charge an hourly fee plus expenses. The hourly rate may differ based on experience, size of the firm, and/or complexity of the project. In some locations, expect to pay a percentage of the cost of the project (the signed contract amount). This could be as much as 18% for a remodeling project or as little as 6% for new construction.

TURN WORDS INTO SPACE

Your Capital Needs Committee should sufficiently prepare basic information for your architect to get started. First, arrange for an up-to-date survey of your property that includes any improvements, the property lines, contour lines, trees, and any easements or set backs upon your land. The legal description is required to obtain a building permit. Not having this information readily available will delay the process.

Needs Assessment

The architect usually conducts a needs assessment by interviewing each member of the staff and committee chair persons. He/she will also meet with the building committee to study the proposed vision. This assessment process assists the architect in better understanding how the building spaces are currently used. The architect will then develop a program for your committee to follow in setting priorities. It will also serve as a checklist throughout the planning process as problems are identified and solutions proposed.

The Design

The architect will work from the written program to produce a schematic design that will later serve as your master plan. He/she is trained to view space in the most efficient way as possible. The Rt. Rev. Jeffery Rowthorn, Episcopal Bishop of the American Convocation in Europe, has remarked: "It has been said that an architect looks at a building and sees what is not there, while the layman looks at the building and sees only what is there."

The architect also has a wealth of experience and knowledge about construction principals and design which will play a large role in the development of your plans. Remember that the architect works every day with building codes, laws, and legal requirements and therefore understands how all of these factors may impact your building design.

Expect to have a series of meetings with the architect where ideas will be presented for your reaction and input. It is this interaction with the architect that will lead to a consensus for the design of the building. As was said in an earlier chapter, the agreed upon design should be shared with all interested people in your congregation. Start with your church leadership, then hold a general meeting with the congregation. Allow the architect to make his/her own presentation. Input from these meetings will enhance the design and the plans will be more accepted once everyone is involved in the process.

The accepted preliminary plan is your master plan and usually includes everything you would like to have built. It should also include the estimated costs of the proposed project. However, can your church afford this vision? This question brings you to the next step—the feasibility study.

Feasibility Study

As noted earlier in this book, a thorough study will provide a great deal of needed information; especially in answering the question, "How much can we raise?" It will allow your committee to set a realistic budget for your program and will help prioritize the elements in your plan according to the responses from your congregation.

After a study, either you will be able to move forward, confident that your vision can become a reality, or you will adjust your plans to correspond with the giving potential of your congregation and constituencies. In many cases, projects are completed with a combination of financial borrowing and capital drives. Ascertain how much debt your congregation can finance and if loans are available at reasonable rates.

Conduct a Capital Campaign

With the feasibility study results and a master plan in place, you can now conduct your capital campaign. With the campaign accomplished and any financing in place, the building process can now proceed.

HIRE A CONSTRUCTION ARCHITECT

You are not required to use the architect who created the master plan for construction. Sometimes a different firm may adopt the master plan concepts and follow the project through to completion. You may have hired the first architect because he/she is a visionary designer, while another architect is recommended as a production oriented professional. You may even choose to have the first architect joint-venture the project with a second architect, joining the visionary artist with a nuts-and-bolts production firm.

The architect will sign an "AIA Contract Between Owner and Architect." This document fully explains what the responsibilities are for each party. It details the phases of the architect's work and is the best resource your committee can review prior to hiring the architect. You can obtain a copy by contacting your local AIA (The American Institute of Architects) office. There is a nominal charge for the document. The following are brief summaries of the work phases:

1. Preliminary Design–The architect will once again review the program requirements and include in the design drawings any legal requirements such as code compliance, handicap accessibility, special considerations for neighbors, etc.

   Remember that constant communication is the key to successfully completing a project. This includes communicating with any adjacent property owners. Sharing development information is not required by law, but it can prevent any misunderstandings that could lead to legal problems and/or objections from neighbors when you apply for a building permit.

2. Design Development–Finishing details such as closets, storage, walls, lighting, and any other special requirements are discussed and put into the plans. This is also when additional engineers become involved in the project for the first time. Your preliminary cost estimate can be reviewed during this phase of the work since the plans will be more complete. The various disciplines can also verify costs for their particular area. The newly detailed cost estimate will allow your committee to review the project and reset priorities accordingly. These final revised plans should be presented to the leadership and the congregation.

3. Construction Documents–Written specifications must be drawn to further define how space is to be divided and used according to the vision of the architect. This phase will result in technical drawings that are less easily read by non-professionals.

   The architect coordinates the work done by all the engineers to create a set of bid documents. The bidding process is similar to hiring an architect. Invite only those contractors whom you would potentially hire. Your architect should be able to recommend appropriate contractor candidates. Many factors should be considered; therefore, rely on your architect's advice.

4. Construction Administration–This is considered by architects to be the key to the successful completion of a project. The architect is again your best guide during this critical part of the project as he/she best understands the overall concept of your building. It is the architect who can tell you whether a proposed material is equal to the one specified in the plans. He/she can also advise you on the percentage of work actually completed so you do not over-pay for construction.

Leaving these details to the architect frees your committee to resolve other problems and considerations. For example, during the construction period, you may be able to move about within your building or you may need to vacate your building altogether. Either way, extra costs should be budgeted.

Planning and building is always a challenge. Working with an architect skilled in church building will make your job as a church leader easier and will ensure that you are being good stewards of the scare funds entrusted to your committee.

Review of the Steps for a Successful Building Project

1. Write a mission statement defining who you are and what you are about as a church.

2. Write a long-range plan articulating the ministries your church wishes to conduct and how they would be accomplished through new construction, renovation or remodeling.

3. Establish a building committee that includes representatives from all groups within the congregation.

4. Employ an architect to create a master plan that turns your words into space and then share these plans with the congregation.

5. Undertake a feasibility study to determine your ability to raise funds.

6. Conduct a capital campaign that, along with possible financing, establishes your achievable budget.

7. Instruct the architect to finalize the plans.

8. Consider other professionals you may need to hire such as an interior designer or landscape architect, etc.

9. Place a bid with a contractor and build the building.

10. Bracket all of the above with prayer for church and congregation as you seek to know and do the will of God.

Epilogue

WE HAVE COVERED MUCH MATERIAL TO THIS POINT. THE TASK BEFORE YOU MAY seem daunting and overwhelming. Remember, however, that each day, church leaders, school heads, and executive directors of church agencies make the critical decision to move forward.

- To restore and renew older facilities.

- To construct new facilities.

- To build endowment for maintenance and programming.

- To find extraordinary funds for new ministries and service.

Remember the example of Moses in the Wilderness when he sought the materials to construct his portable temple. Seek to know first what God would have you to do. Then using those God-given talents of organization, communication, and the ability to lead, go forth to accomplish increased ministry and service in your time and place.

If we are about the work of God, and if people have heard the word of God, then faithful people will respond "with generous hearts."